# MARIJUANA

# marijuana

## facts,
## figures
## and information
## for the 1980's

**Brent Q. Hafen, Ph.D.**
Dept. of Health Sciences
Brigham Young University

**Kathryn J. Frandsen**
Research Associate

First Published, Jan., 1980
Second Printing November, 1981

ISBN: 0-89486-073-9

Printed in the United States of America

Editor's Note:
   Hazelden Educational Materials offers a variety of information on chemical dependency and related areas. Our publications do not necessarily represent Hazelden or its programs, nor do they officially speak for any Twelve Step organization.

# CONTENTS

# HISTORY

As a result of a long and intimate association with man, strange things often happen to plants. They travel around the world; they grow in strange (and often inhospitable) places where the soils and environments are completely foreign to their natural habitats. They often hybridize. As man interacts with them, characteristics that are associated with specific uses may be altered by selection. In some cases, they may escape cultivation altogether and become, ultimately, weeds. In still other cases they become economically important as a crop or agent of value for medicinal purposes.

A primary example of a plant that has, through history, undergone varied roles in relationship to man is *Cannabis* — known in the United States as marijuana. Over a period spanning thousands of years, marijuana has been cultivated by men in many cultures for hempen fibers, for its oil, for its seeds (which were, in some cultures, used as food), for its narcotic properties, and for its therapeutic properties.[1] Evidence indicates that *Cannabis* is probably man's oldest cultivated source of fiber; additional sources indicate that it is the first fiber source to have spread so rapidly and so widely.

The first evidence of *Cannabis* use dates back 5,000 years to China and Chinese Turkestan, where Neolithic men made thread and rope from the hemp of the marijuana plant. The oldest known name for *Cannabis* is *ta-ma*: Chinese for *hemp*.

1

The Chinese character for the word represents the plants growing near a house, which would suggest that the earliest and most important use of the plant was in the home. The Chinese believe that the emperor Shen Nung — the inventor of agriculture and the patron of medicine — cultivated marijuana as early as 2800 B.C. and taught its cultivation to his students that year. Fabrics fashioned of hemp fibers have been excavated from Turkish sites dated to 800 B.C. and from an Egyptian tomb believed to be between 3,000 and 4,000 years old.

The Scythians, who originated in the Altai Mountains in central Asia, grew *Cannabis* for its fiber; the garments fashioned from the hemp closely resembled linen.

*Cannabis* arrived in Europe from the north, with hemp for ropes and sails imported into Sicily from Gaul as early as 300 B.C. Before the birth of Christ, Greeks and Romans did not cultivate *Cannabis* themselves, but instead relied on imports from surrounding areas. The Roman writer, Lucilius, mentioned the plant and its use for rope and sails in writings dating back to 120 B.C.

The first evidence of marijuana's narcotic use was recorded by Herodotus, who reported that the Scythians threw the seeds of *Cannabis* onto a bed of hot stones in an enclosed area and became intoxicated as they breathed the vapors.

As a commercial product valued for its hemp and its oils, *Cannabis* was widely manufactured in Europe after the birth of Christ. Pliny the Elder, the Roman historian, details how hempen fibers were prepared and graded; a Roman fort in England dated A.D. 140–180 yielded hempen rope, indicating that hemp was introduced to the British Isles by Romans coming from Gaul.

Pollen studies indicate that *Cannabis* was widely cutivated in Europe from A.D. 400 to A.D. 1100. Apparently the Vikings used it, either for ropes or sails, because hempen fishing lines and fabrics have been found in Viking graves in Norway, and the plant was widely grown in Iceland throughout the Middle Ages. After its introduction to England, *Cannabis* was planted as a result of royal decree from England's King Henry VIII. English farmers continued cultivation of hemp, and during Elizabethan times England's maritime supremacy created such a demand for hemp that its cultivation spread to the New World.

Cultivation of hemp was first introduced in North America at Port Royal, Canada, in 1606. The first crop was planted in Virginia in 1611, and the Pilgrims brought marijuana to Plymouth in 1632. The fiber was used in pre-Revolutionary America to make clothing and fabric for other uses, and the colonists exported the crop to England for use in sails, rope, and fabrics.

*Cannabis* never became a major crop in the Spanish and Portuguese colonies of the New World, even though it was introduced in Chile as early as 1545 and seeds sent from Spain arrived in Peru in 1554.

While the crop did not assume importance in South America, it became increasingly important in the United States. Extensive hemp plantations flourished in the area surrounding Kentucky and enjoyed great prosperity until the disruption of the Civil War — which brought with it rising labor costs — killed the industry in the late nineteenth century. By the late 1870s little hemp was being produced commercially in the United States, but the seeds from the plantations had spread, and the plant was found as a weed in the Middle Atlantic and New England states.

Hemp fiber is today produced mainly in Poland and Russia; hemp of the finest quality comes from Spain and Italy. Hemp as a crop is not commercially important in the United States.

Cultivation of hemp (*Cannabis*) for its oil — first evidenced in Germany in about 500 B.C. — continues on a small scale in Russia and eastern Europe. The oil is used as a substitute for linseed oil in the paint and varnish industry, in soap making, and as a lubricant. In some areas of Russia, the oil is used in lamps to light homes. Part of the oil, which has drying properties, is used in the production of emulsions for pharmaceutical products.

As a food, *Cannabis* was cultivated earlier than it was for hemp. Rich in fat, the roasted seeds have been used widely by a number of different peoples, especially in times of famine. The mature seeds are devoid of intoxicating properties and are still eaten today in eastern Europe. They are valued today in the United States as a feed ingredient for birds and poultry.

Perhaps the most controversial and historically interesting aspect of *Cannabis* has been its use as a narcotic or medicine. The medicinal value of hemp is its most significant, and *Cannabis* is one of the world's major medicinal plants. Shen Nung, the legendary Chinese emperor mentioned earlier, prescribed marijuana as a medicinal cure for beriberi, malaria, rheumatism, constipation, absentmindedness, and female disorders as early as 5,000 years ago — the first recorded evidence of the use of *Cannabis* as medicine. A contemporary of Shen Nung, Chinese physician Hoa-Gho, used a mixture of hemp resin and wine to deaden pain during surgery — one of the first recorded uses of anesthesia.

Hemp was valued in ancient India as a gift from the gods that would lower fevers, relieve dysentery, stimulate the appetite, foster sleep, prolong life, quicken the mind, improve judgment, and cure a myriad of miscellaneous ills. Because of its narcotic and hallucinogenic properties, *Cannabis* was valued in ancient India as a much more mysterious — and therefore important — medicine than those medicines having merely physical properties.

Several prominent Indian medical volumes detail the use of marijuana. The *Sushruta* recommends marijuana as a cure for leprosy, as an antiphlegmatic, and as a treatment for catarrh when accompanied by diarrhea. Marijuana was described as antiphlegmatic, bile affecting, astringent, pungent, and digestive in the *Bhavaprakasha*, an Indian medical volume written about A.D. 1600. The same volume recommends the use of marijuana in the treatment of digestive disorders and recommends it to arouse the appetite and strengthen the voice. Indian medicine hailed marijuana in the treatment of dandruff, headache, gonorrhea, whooping cough, earache, consumption, insomnia, and mania. It is still used in India today as a medicine.

As cultivation of *Cannabis* spread, so did its fame as a medicine. As it spread into Africa, hemp was used as the preferred drug in treating tropical fevers, malaria, anthrax, and dysentery. Today, marijuana is considered in Africa as the most versatile and varied medicine available; it is used as a remedy for snakebite by members of both the Mfengu and Hottentot tribes. Sotho women partially stupefy themselves prior to childbirth by smoking marijuana.

*Cannabis* reached the pinnacle of its importance as a medicine in Europe, where it was valued both as a professional and a folk medication. Europeans differentiated between the cultivated and wild plant; the wild plant was not widely used except as a treatment for nodes and tumors. The cultivated hemp (called "manured hempe") was used in a variety of ways to treat a variety of ills. Crushed in white wine, it was used to relieve the symptoms of jaundice. Boiled in milk, the seeds were used to treat hot, dry cough. Fed to hens, the seeds were thought to increase egg-laying. Poured into holes in the ground, marijuana decoctions drew earthworms to the surface, which fishermen then used to bait their hooks. In ancient Asia, fishermen used parts of the plant on their hooks, since marijuana apparently stupefied the fish.

As the plant spread to Europe and was used medicinally, some practitioners warned of its side effects. In 1640, Parkinson warned that marijuana caused respiratory problems and led to sterility. A few years earlier, Dodoens had in 1619 asserted that marijuana led to sterility ("drieth up . . . the saede of generation") and that it "drieth up the milke of women's breasts."

Modern European and American medicine did not take a serious interest in marijuana until the nineteenth century; during the latter half of that century, more than a hundred articles on its use appeared in medical journals. *Cannabis* was widely used in the form of a tincture to cure insomnia, to calm nervous restlessness, and to act as an analgesic. Today it is used in limited cases to reduce the pain of migraine headache. Because marijuana is difficult to standardize and because individual doses are difficult to determine, *Cannabis* preparations are not available as medicine in the United States today. It appeared in the United States Pharmacopoeia and the National Formulary until 1937, but it has been dropped from the lists of official drugs in both the United States and Europe.

Of course, the most controversial and significant aspect of *Cannabis* is its euphoric and hallucinogenic property, and its use as a narcotic dates back almost as far as its use as a hemp fiber.

As early as 5,000 years ago, China's Sheng Nung recognized *Cannabis*'s narcotic properties when he recommended it as a medicine — and one of marijuana's Chinese names means, literally, "liberator of sin." A later Chinese name meant "delight giver," an obvious reflection of marijuana's intoxicating effect. Following a report that eating hemp would cause the user to see spirits, the Chinese were using *Cannabis* for "enjoyment of life."

West of China lived the barbarian tribes of Asia, who undoubtedly were responsible for the spread of *Cannabis* as a narcotic. Among those people were the Scythians, who inhaled the intoxicating fumes of *Cannabis* seeds placed on hot rocks. The Sythians, who wandered widely in southeast Europe and central Asia, had a profound influence on the cultural development of early Greece and eastern Europe, and they brought with them the intoxicating *Cannabis*.

One of the most sacred plants in India was *Cannabis*, and bhang (a decoction made from powdered hemp fermented in milk or water) was used to cleanse the user of sin and to deter evil. A pilgrim from India introduced the narcotic to Persia during the reign of Khusru (A.D. 531−579), and prior to that time the Assyrians had used hemp as an incense.

The use of *Cannabis* as an inebriating narcotic spread gradually across Asia Minor; the pressed, pure resin from the top of the *Cannabis* plant — hashish — is referred to obscurely in several sections of the Old Testament.

Hashish, though originally prohibited among the Islamic people, spread widely and rapidly. Government officials in 1378 imposed harsh penalties for eating hashish, but their efforts to stop its use were in vain. Hashish was so well known that Marco Polo in 1271 described its use among certain groups who used the narcotic to experience the rewards in store for them in the afterlife. One such group — the Hashashins — was under the leadership of a fanatic named Hasan-Ibn-Sabbah, who enticed followers to assassinate political enemies in return for a drink containing *Cannabis* resin. (The word *assassin* came into European languages from the word *hashashin*, meaning "eaters of hashish.")

While the early Greeks and Romans used *Cannabis* as a medicine, its use as an intoxicant or narcotic was rare until the first century A.D., when Romans started eating cakes containing hashish to promote hilarity.

As *Cannabis* spread into Africa, a number of tribes in the Zambezi Valley began inhaling the vapors from piles of smouldering hemp; later they fashioned pipes from reeds and began smoking the hemp. Today, the Kasai tribes of the Congo have revived an ancient tribal ceremony in which hemp has become a god, a protector against both spiritual and physical harm. Business transactions and treaties are sealed with a puff of smoke, and in many tribes throughout Africa, hemp-smoking and hashish-sniffing cults are active today.

*Cannabis* was not used as a narcotic in the New World until recently, when Mexican laborers in Texas in the late 1910s introduced the smoking of marijuana. By the 1920s the habit was firmly established in New Orleans, where its use was mainly confined to the poor — especially to members of minority groups. In 1937, with the use of *Cannabis* spreading rapidly among Americans, the Marijuana Tax Act made it illegal to grow or possess *Cannabis*.

Today, there are an estimated 200 to 300 million *Cannabis* users throughout the world; most are located in Asia, the Middle East, and North Africa.

## Derivatives of Marijuana

Two major derivatives of marijuana — hashish and hashish oil — have become prominent on the illicit drug scene.

Ten to twenty times more potent than the American varieties of marijuana, hashish is made from the crude resin of the *Cannabis* plant. The highest quality hashish ("hash") is made by scraping the resin from the plant with a piece of leather; the resin, a brownish color, darkens with age and is sold in sticks or small lumps.

Less refined hashish is harvested by threshing and drying the cut *Cannabis* plants; dried brown-green or brown-gray hashish falls like dust from the plants and is collected in cloth bags, which are flattened and pressed and stacked into "soles."

A still less refined product is obtained by pressing the sticky plant tops between coarse cloth; the resin sticks to the cloth, and is graded by color.

Usually smoked, hashish can also be brewed into a strong tea or eaten (cooked into a confectionary).

Much more potent than conventional forms of hashish, hashish oil has recently begun to be marketed on the illicit drug market. While hashish contains 10 percent delta-9-THC (the most potent psychoactive ingredient in marijuana), hashish oil contains anywhere from 22 to 70 percent delta-9-THC.

## Uses of Marijuana

As described in the historical analysis of marijuana use, the plant itself has been cultivated for centuries for fiber and seed. The seed is still used today in a variety of ways: as a bird feed ingredient, as a cattle feed ingredient, and, when pressed for oil, in paint and soap manufacturing.

In many countries of the world, marijuana is still an important element of folk medicine; as explained later in this monograph, it is currently being studied for its benefits in treating a number of diseases and disorders.

Marijuana is probably used most widely in India, where it is popular in three forms: *bhang* (a weak drink made from the cut tops of the *Cannabis* plant), *ganja* (a product made from the resin of the flowering tops of female plants, and which is smoked or eaten), and *charas* (a product made directly from resin and smoked).

# EXTENT OF USE [2]

An official government report released in 1977 revealed that 11 percent — nearly four million in all — high school seniors in the United States were smoking marijuana every day.[3] In a report issued by the same agency in 1978, the National Institute on Drug Abuse reported that marijuana use in the United States had climbed 25 percent in just one year.

The sharpest rise in users was among the twelve to seventeen age group; the second sharpest rise was among those ages eighteen to twenty-five. Over one in four of the latter age group use marijuana regularly. The use of marijuana continues to be strongly related to age: only 7 percent of those aged thirty-five have ever even *tried* marijuana.

The greatest percentage of users, according to the 1978 report, were those in high school: the 1978 high school seniors nationwide reported that one in eleven of them smoked marijuana daily.

Statistics released by the Department of Health, Education, and Welfare in 1975 indicate that the use of *Cannabis* among Americans is increasing sharply. A majority (53 percent) of those between the ages of eighteen and twenty-five have tried marijuana; almost one in four under the age of eighteen has experimented with the drug. Of those under eighteen, 12 percent regularly used the drug in 1975. One-third of current users indicated their future plans to continue using the drug.

Marijuana use is not as pronounced among Americans over

the age of twenty-five: while over half of those younger have tried *Cannabis*, only a third of the older population have experimented with marijuana. The older the age group, the less common marijuana usage: of those over the age of thirty-five, less than one in one hundred use the drug regularly. This trend may not continue, however, since over half of America's college students use marijuana regularly, and over a third of those who do use it plan to continue using it.

Marijuana has lost some of its nontraditional and nonconservative stigma, with the result that its users come from all classes, socio-economic groups, and ages. Current government estimates for 1979 conclude that 43 million Americans have smoked marijuana at least once, and the number of current users exceeds 16 million.[4]

# PHARMACOLOGY

The most common method of using marijuana is by smoking dried plant parts, mostly the leaves and flowers. A less common, but still widespread method of drug use involves eating the plant parts (usually mixed in cakes, breads, brownies, or some other food). Eating provides a slower effect, but temperatures required for baking alter the chemistry of the *Cannabis*, resulting in stronger, more potent drug actions.

Generally those who smoke marijuana also smoke cigarettes, since the technique of drawing smoke into the lungs is dependent on practice and skill — usually obtained through cigarette smoking.

Some attempts have been made at mulching the plant parts and injecting them intravenously, but such a method of administration is dangerous, even fatal because of clots that form in the substance which may subsequently lodge in the lungs.

In India, the plant parts are still concocted into a strong drink called *bhang*. Using the drug as a drink is rare in other cultures.

The chemical constituents of the *Cannabis* plant include a specific and unique group of chemicals called the cannabinoids. As far as potency is concerned, the five most important cannabinoids are delta-9-THC (delta-9-trans-tetrahydrocannabinol), delta-8-THC, THC-acid (delta-9-trans-tetrahydrocannabinolic acid), CBN (cannabinol), and CBD (cannabidiol).[5]

The main ingredient — and the one that causes the major

12

psychoactive reaction — in *Cannabis* is delta-9-THC; the other four ingredients listed above (and still other negligible ingredients) have little biologic effect.[6]

Smoking the dried and chopped stems, leaves, and flowers of the *Cannabis* plant, as mentioned earlier, provides the most effective administration; the amount of delta-9-THC absorbed into the bloodstream from the lungs varies considerably among smokers, but major psychoactive and physiologic effects usually appear within two to three minutes (and sometimes less).[7] The peak effect occurs within ten to twenty minutes, and the psychoactive and physiologic effects last from ninety to one hundred-twenty minutes. Approximately 5 mg. of delta-9-THC is contained in one marijuana cigarette.

Onset of effects is slower when the plant parts are eaten (either alone or as part of a confectionary). Onset begins thirty to sixty minutes after ingestion; the peak is reached two to three hours following eating, and the effects last three to five hours. When administration is oral — that is, when the plant parts are eaten in some form — three times as much marijuana is required to produce the effects obtained from smoking.

Almost all of the delta-9-THC is metabolized by the body: less than 1 percent is found unchanged in the urine or feces of those who use marijuana, regardless of whether the *Cannabis* is smoked, ingested, or drunk. Once in the bloodstream, delta-9-THC is rapidly transformed into 11-hydroxy-THC (11-OH-THC), a compound as potent as the parent delta-9-THC. The 11-OH-THC is then transformed quickly into the inactive 8, 11-dihydroxy-THC. During the metabolizing process, delta-9-THC is bound to lipoproteins in the blood (and, therefore, is found in high concentrations in the body's fatty tissues), while the 11-OH-THC is bound to albumin. As the two chemicals disappear from the bloodstream, they are distributed to the various body organs, where they accumulate: delta-9-THC to the lungs, salivary glands, jejunum, kidneys, adrenal glands, muscles, liver, and testes (in decreasing order of concentration levels), with high concentrations found in the brain for the first seven days following inhalation or ingestion; 11-OH-THC remains bound to the albumin.

After the initial distribution to various body organs, relatively high concentrations of radioactivity are found in the liver, the bile, the gastrointestinal tract, the kidneys, and the bladder. The delta-9-THC can cross the placenta in pregnant women, resulting in sizable concentrations of delta-9-THC in the fetus.

While 99 percent of the delta-9-THC is metabolized by the body, the 1 percent that is not metabolized — the metabolic waste — is excreted through the urine and feces, with radioactive traces visible in the urine and feces for days after the administration of a single large dose (making it possible for forensic teams to detect the presence of marijuana with much greater accuracy than the presence of alcohol).

The presence of delta-9-THC in the body affects the heart rate, the intraocular pressure, and the color of the conjunctiva; it has no apparent effect on the body temperature, respiratory rate, or deep tendon reflexes. It has no apparent effect on blood sugar or plasma levels and has a minute effect on pupillary size.

When marijuana is fresh — before it is dried or altered in any way — 95 percent of the THC exists in acidic form, which is not active in producing intoxicating effects.[8] As the plant is dried, the acid slowly decarboxylates (losing its acid properties), forming THC; the process can be speeded up by heat (either through smoking, exposure to sunlight, or baking).

While the average marijuana cigarette contains between 2.5 and 5 mg. delta-9-THC, the amount varies greatly depending on where the plant was grown, which part of the plant is used to make the cigarette, and which generation the plant comes from. Mexican marijuana — plants grown in Mexico — is more potent than marijuana grown in the United States, and the first-generation plants provide the greatest concentration of delta-9-THC — as do the flowers and leaves of the plants.

Because delta-9-THC is poorly absorbed through the intestine, marijuana has more intoxicating properties when it is smoked rather than ingested. In addition, certain elements in the *Cannabis* plant are activated through the combustion process of smoking.

Whether smoked or eaten, there is a wide variability in the potency of different parts of the *Cannabis* plant. Both sexes of the plant contain about the same amount of the most active ingredient (delta-9-THC); there is little delta-9-THC in the leaves, large stems, and roots. Most of the psychoactive ingredient is found in the flowers, pollen, small leaves, and small stems. The highest concentration of delta-9-THC — up to 11 percent — is found in the small leaves next to the flower (the bracts).

Uncultivated American varieties of marijuana are generally quite weak; varieties grown in Vietnam, Nepal, Africa, Mexico, and India are the strongest available. (Recent studies have revealed that seed origin probably has more to do with potency than does location: Mexican seed transplanted in Mississippi, for instance, retains the potency of the Mexican marijuana grown in Mexico.)

# REASONS FOR USE

While each person's reason for using *Cannabis* varies a little from each other person's reason, certain patterns have developed that lead to some commonalities for use of the drug.

Reasons for *starting* to use the drug (or for experimenting with marijuana) include the desire for a pleasurable feeling, the desire to escape from tensions, curiosity as to the effects, and association with other users (who often exert peer pressure).[9] Some who start to use marijuana are looking for a substitute (or permanent replacement) for some other drug — such as alcohol, cocaine, opium, or a number of common tranquilizers. In some cultures (such as that in India), religious or medical practices lead a user to start.

*Continuing* to use the drug is due to some of the same reasons as apply to starting to use the drug — most specifically a relief from tension, a replacement for another drug, or peer pressure and association with other users. Other reasons for continued use include enhancement of sexual satisfaction; increased enjoyment of music or food; alleviation of hunger; relief from boredom or frustration; relief from depression; enhancement of creative abilities; attainment of mystical states (especially applicable to members of religious cults); enhancement of meditation; and boosting of courage. The religious use of *Cannabis* is common in India, Brazil, Jamaica, Mexico, and Africa.

Social reasons are extremely important; more than any other

intoxicant, *Cannabis* is used throughout the world in small social settings, and *Cannabis* use provides the user with an intimate sense of belonging — a factor that leads to both experimentation and continued use. While *Cannabis* users differ widely in personal sociocultural backgrounds and extent of use, they tend to share certain characteristics. Use is closely related to age, with adolescents and young adults making up the majority of users. Except in Europe and North America, females rarely use *Cannabis*; even in Europe and North America, men use marijuana much more frequently than do women.

The illegal status of marijuana contributes to the fact that its use is frowned upon, and this factor has until recently delegated its use to members of lower socioeconomic groups. More recent developments have led to the use of marijuana among members of all socioeconomic groups, although use is still heaviest among lower-class members.

*Cannabis* users in general share certain personality characteristics: they prefer an unstructured and spontaneous life-style; they are relatively prone to take risks; they value states of altered consciousness; and they tend to seek states of altered consciousness through methods other than drugs (in addition to the use of drugs).

The characteristic *Cannabis* user is a young, unmarried male who evidences some instability in residence, employment, education, and long-term goals. Excessive users often evidence personality inadequacies including: emotional immaturity, low frustration tolerance, and a failure to assume responsibility.

Those who experiment briefly with *Cannabis* and who discontinue use, or those who decide not to use *Cannabis* at all (with no experimentation experience) tend to prefer a controlled, structured, rational, and secure life-style.

Some sociocultural reasons may promote marijuana use among those who would not normally use it (or may increase marijuana use among casual or experimental users): rapid industrialization; rapid urbanization; social conflict; or transition between war and peace. In such circumstances, an individual's system of values may be changing; affiliation with new peers and separation from family and established friends may remove normal restraints on behavior. Some sociocultural changes — especially rapid industrialization or urbanization — may result in increased pressures that lead to use. For instance, a peasant in a Bolivian village may use marijuana only occasionally but may increase his use sharply after moving to a city slum where filth, disease, and crowded living conditions add stresses to one's life-style.

# EFFECTS [10]

When marijuana use first became widespread in the late 1960s, advocates argued that it had few (if any) physical effects, and that its psychological effects were short-term only (as in the case of simple intoxication). Recent efforts by medical researchers, however, have revealed evidence of long-term physical and psychological effects, some of which lead to permanent damage both mentally and physically.

## Physical Effects

Any form of drug abuse will have more devastating effects on individuals who are especially vulnerable — and children and adolescents are among the group of those considered inherently more vulnerable. Children and adolescents, who are still in various stages of physical and psychological development, suffer more pronounced and persistent effects from *Cannabis* use than do adults, but the following effects are common to all age groups. Their severity and intensity will probably vary according to the age, health, and general vulnerability of the user. A person who is already ill or who is suffering from a chronic disease will always suffer more intense effects from *Cannabis* use.

## Effects on the Brain

Because of the metabolization of delta-9-THC and its tendency to accumulate in the fatty tissues, marijuana accumulates

19

in concentrated amounts in the brain tissue; significant amounts can be found in the brain up to eight days after ingestion. (No other drug has yet been found to have such long-lasting results.)

Findings on the effect of marijuana on the brain are not clear-cut and are subject to some controversy, but the results of some experiments conducted in the United States and in England indicate that marijuana leads to significant atrophy of brain tissue.

During intoxication, significant changes in the normal EEG pattern of brain activity occur, but the long-range implications of such brain-activity pattern change is not known. Currently, X-ray techniques have not conclusively shown permanent damage to brain tissue.

Some effects of intoxication are also being discussed as possible permanent effects — including loss of memory, slow-down of the learning process, and inability to control motor and involuntary motor processes. Marijuana use also leads to a dulling of time perception, depth perception, distance perception, and speed perception — all of which affect the ability to drive safely.

Other long-term effects on the brain function include upset in motor coordination, causing a change in gait, uncontrolled laughter, a lag between thought and facial expressions, and unsteady hands. Once thought to be only temporary effects of intoxication, research has proven that these effects may in many cases be long-term and may increase as frequency of marijuana use increases.

Marijuana use also affects the deep control centers located in the brain. Users find that marijuana causes the white of the eyes to turn red, facial skin to turn red, pupils to dilate (making the eyes extremely sensitive to light), appetite to increase or decrease markedly, mouth and throat to get excessively dry, extremities to grow cold, and symptoms of nausea, vomiting, and diarrhea to develop. (These changes in the deep control centers also cause many psychological effects, which will be discussed later in this section.)

Marijuana residue tends to accumulate in greater concentrations in the brain's gray matter than in the white matter, with resulting impairment in abstract thinking. Subjects who have used marijuana heavily over a prolonged period of time are unable to distinguish between abstract and concrete thinking — a syndrome called "marijuana thinking."

Accumulation of delta-9-THC in the fatty tissues of the brain may cause literal destruction of brain cells and literal dissolution of the thin membranes critical in preserving brain structure. Damaged cells cannot be replaced; in some cases, alternate pathways around destroyed cells can be formed through the brain. In many cases, users make adjustments for chemical disturbances and brain cell destruction.

Studies involving a number of healthy young male subjects who had smoked marijuana heavily over a long period of time showed brain atrophy comparable to that found normally in ninety-year-old men. The brain damage is progressive — cannabinoids accumulated in the brain take so long to be eliminated that atrophy continues long after marijuana use is discontinued. This progressive atrophy is responsible for the psychic changes that accompany marijuana use (discussed later in this section).

Still other studies involving healthy young male long-term users indicated that brain atrophy results in literal shrinkage of the cerebral structures; study subjects had lost the fluid in the inner cavity of the brain, and that fluid had been replaced with air.

Brain damage has also been evidenced in moderate users of marijuana. Those who smoked two marijuana cigarettes a day for a period of two years suffered major disturbances in brain wave activity; those disturbances (measured by an EEG) corresponded to behavioral and mental changes. Even among moderate users — those who had used marijuana for up to two years

— the effects were observed up to two years after discontinued use.

Marijuana also disturbs blood flow in the brain. Cerebral blood flow is *not* uniform — the two parts of the brain that receive (and require) the greatest blood flow are the cerebral cortex and the deep brain area, which require up to four times the amount of blood required by the other sections of the brain. Those two areas — the cerebral cortex and the deep brain area — are also the two areas most affected by marijuana, and accumulation of delta-9-THC in those areas causes tissue starvation due to inadequate blood flow. If continued over a period of time, such tissue starvation leads to cell destruction and brain tissue atrophy.

Because the brain controls all body systems, the effect of marijuana on the brain also affects all other body systems — some generally, and some more specifically.

## Effects on Cells

Moderate use of marijuana — smoking of as few as three cigarettes a week — may seriously interfere with the body's production of RNA and DNA in the cells. Reduction of RNA and DNA synthesis sharply reduces the mitotic index, or the rate at which the cells give birth to new cells. Use even three times a week can result in a 41 percent reduction of new cell production.

Slowing down the body's vital DNA production may lead to two conditions: chromosome breakage and breakdown of the body's immune response system.

Studies at the University of Utah Medical Center revealed that more than 60 percent of those who used marijuana moderately suffered a significant number of chromosome breaks — up to three times as many as nonusers. Unfortunately, since marijuana use has been widespread for only a decade, and because the heaviest use has been among adolescents, the incidence of possible birth defects has yet to be witnessed. Results of studies lead to the conclusion that such birth defects may become evident.

Marijuana's interference with the body's production of DNA also lowers resistance to disease, disrupting the body's immune response system. Immune-globulin G, a chemical vital to immunity, has been found to be reduced among moderate marijuana users. T-lymphocytes, also critical to immunity, are destroyed by marijuana and can be destroyed in those who smoke one to three cigarettes a week for a period of at least one year. Moderate marijuana users are more likely to be affected by disease and are less likely to be able to fight off disease than are nonusers. Among those who use marijuana heavily, the tendency to develop disease can be 68 percent higher.

Implications of DNA and RNA destruction run deeper than just possible chromosome damage to offspring and increased susceptibility to disease. The chromosomes carry the genetic information for each cell, and that genetic information is passed not only to offspring but to each new cell that is formed within the body. Each new cell (with rare exceptions) is identical to the cell from which it was derived. Marijuana use (as little as twice a week) can lead to chromosome breakage that affects the cells manufactured in the body, leading to mutations, tumors, virus disease, anemia, and early aging. Normally, chromosomes break at a very low rate; this rate is accelerated sharply by exposure to radiation, certain viruses, and toxic chemicals (including delta-9-THC).

Studies have recently indicated that marijuana use causes the chromosome breakage that occurs normally as a part of the aging process. Moderate use of marijuana can cause as much chromosome breakage in two years as would normally occur in fifty years.

Marijuana's effects on production of RNA and DNA is apparently a result of the drug's deterioration of the cell's outer membranes.

*Effect on Pregnancy and Offspring*

Marijuana use has been shown to effect both male and female reproductive systems and to have serious implications for the health of the fetus during pregnancy.

Smoking two marijuana cigarettes a day can disturb the level of ovarian hormones and can interfere with the ovarian cycle in as few as twelve days of use. Marijuana use can also lead to early menopause, triggering hormone levels that cause menopause onset to be six times as high as in nonusers.

Marijuana also has deleterious effects on levels and production of testosterone — the hormone that causes development of facial hair, development of muscle tissue, and development of the reproductive system in the male. Researchers are unsure about the permanency of this effect, and some studies indicate that testosterone levels return to normal shortly after discontinuance of the drug.

Evidence also suggests that long-term marijuana use may lead to a decrease in the tissue mass of the testes, resulting in interference with testosterone production as well as sperm production. Sperm count is lower among users of marijuana than among nonusers; in 35 percent of the users the sperm count was low enough to render the users sterile. Marijuana users in general had a 44 percent lower testosterone level than did nonusers.

Sperm may also be destroyed or altered by marijuana. Studies of marijuana users reveal that delta-9-THC may cause degeneration of sperm, fragmentation of sperm, and improper sperm formation due to impairment of protein synthesis critical to the formation of the head of the sperm. The question is: Can sperm fragmentation lead to damage in the offspring?

Delta-9-THC and other chemicals (most of them toxic) found in marijuana accumulate in high concentrations in the placenta and embryonic tissue, causing a reduction in birth weight and a sharp increase in the incidence of stillbirths. Fetal death and fetal abnormality have been shown to be directly related to marijuana use, and the severity of fetal abnormality (and incidence of fetal death) is directly related to the doses and frequency of marijuana used by the mother.

Nursing babies of mothers who use marijuana are also subject to all of the toxic effects of marijuana. Such babies suffer physical damage as well as a marked decline in mental vigor. Marijuana can be detected in infants who are nursing as short as four hours after the mother inhaled or ingested the *Cannabis*.

## *Effects on the Lungs*

Users who smoke large amounts of marijuana over long periods of time are subject to chronic bronchitis and severe emphysema. Studies involving American soldiers who had smoked up to thirty grams of marijuana a month over the period of six to fifteen months showed that they had developed destruction of lung tissue that requires twenty years or more of tobacco smoking to develop.

Because marijuana must be inhaled deeply and held longer in the lungs than tobacco smoke, the lungs of marijuana users are more blackened than the lungs of tobacco smokers. The concentration of delta-9-THC is greater in the lungs than in any other body tissue, and examination reveals serious breakdown in lung tissue among marijuana users.

In normal, quiet breathing, air is not drawn into the small air sacs, but is drawn instead only into the smaller airway tubes (bronchioles) that ventilate the air sacs. The modules of oxygen and carbon dioxide rapidly diffuse between the air sacs and the air tubes during normal breathing; nicotine, which enters the lungs on particles of tobacco cigarette smoke, dissociates readily with the oxygen and enters the bloodstream without needing to be drawn into the air sacs. But THC is tightly bound to the surface of the carbon particles; those carbon particles must be deeply inhaled into the lungs, where they are drawn into the air sacs and held until they adhere to the walls of the air sacs next to microscopic capillaries that feed the air sacs. Over the period of several minutes the THC molecules are absorbed from the carbon particles directly into the bloodstream.

Almost half of those who smoke marijuana suffer from chronic sore throat, laryngitis, and pharyngitis. The same amount suffer from respiratory diseases; a few less have chronic bronchitis and emphysema. Some suffer from restrictive lung disease (such as interstitial fibrosis), and all suffer some impairment of lung function.

Over a long term, marijuana use leads to degeneration of the cell nuclei in the lungs, and can result in a condition leading to lung cancer. (A number of subjects were found to have lung cancer that exactly duplicated the lung cancer resulting from tobacco smoke.) Long-term use also results in tissue destruction (necrosis) and in destruction of the membranous linings of the lungs.

## Effect on Liver

Because many marijuana users also drink alcohol, it is difficult to determine how much liver damage is caused by marijuana and how much is caused by alcohol. In one study of marijuana users who did not use alcohol or who used alcohol in only moderate and infrequent doses, definite liver damage was indicated by biopsy in those who had smoked marijuana for two to six years. A study of those who had smoked marijuana for six months to two years showed little damage to the liver and little (if any) impairment of liver function, leading to the conclusion that liver damage results only after years (instead of months) of marijuana use.

## Effect on the Heart

While marijuana does not lead to the development of heart disease in normal, healthy young adults, it can lead to the onset of critical heart problems in those who had a tendency for heart disease or in those whose hearts were less than healthy. Particularly serious is the result of lowering the exercise tolerance in those who have the anginal syndrome.

When administered in high doses, marijuana can cause a lowering of blood pressure (probably due to its effects on the central nervous system instead of on the heart muscle itself). High doses of marijuana can also cause racing of the heart (sharply increased heart rate), but the heart beat generally returns to normal after discontinuance of use. In most cases, cardiac output is decreased during use.

## Other Physical Effects

Moderate marijuana use also causes an inability of the blood to be properly oxygenated, abnormal dilation or constriction of pupils, decrease of intraocular pressure, decrease in body temperature, weight gain (due to increase in appetite and decrease in physical exercise), increase of REM sleep, and reduction of sympathetic nerve activity.

## Psychological Effects

While marijuana's physical effects have not been widely acknowledged among users, its psychological effects are acknowledged and hailed — and, in many cases, are the reason for the use.

Marijuana users themselves report vivid changes in sensation, including ability to see patterns, forms, figures, or meaningful designs in visual material that normally has no particular form; ability to visualize objects more sharply; ability to see things in three-dimensional depth; visualization of new colors or shades of color; acquisition of a sensual quality to vision that makes it seem as though the user can "touch" an object he is looking at; the ability to hear more subtle changes in sounds; the ability to understand song lyrics that are usually unclear; ability to hear greater spatial separation between musical instruments; vivid auditory images; variance in the sound quality of the user's voice; more exciting, sensual sense of touch; increase in the heaviness of objects; increase in taste sensations; increased enjoyment of eating; craving of sweets; increase in sense of smell; and increase in the distance between the user and other objects or people.

Marijuana users claim a different feeling toward their own body, describing a "pleasant warmth" inside the body; awareness of the beating of the heart; feeling of lightness, as if the user were floating in midair; a feeling of flowing energy in the body; awareness of air filling the lungs; ability to tolerate pain easily; and a tingling or vibration in the body.

Users also describe an effect on physical movement, saying that their emotions seem exceptionally well-coordinated with their physical movement. In connection with interpersonal relations, users say that they experience deep insight into other people, difficulty in playing ordinary social games, tremendous empathy, feelings of isolation, and desires to interact more with people. Most describe increase in the intensity of orgasm and increase in the enjoyment of love-making.

Much less acclaimed by users are the less pleasant psychological effects of marijuana: antisocial behavior, reduction of attention span, propensity toward mental illness, schizophrenia, mania, personality deterioration, loss of motivation, inability to form normal thought processes, inability to concentrate, loss of affection for loved ones (including family members), loss of inhibition (leading in many cases to urination in public places), loss of willpower, paranoia, and loss of learning ability.

Study of the psychological effects of marijuana use have led researchers to identify the "cannabis syndrome," a behavior disorder characterized by "diminished drive, lessened ambition, decreased motivation, and apathy." Mental tasks requiring concentration and attention — specifically the ability to read — are greatly impaired among those who use marijuana.

Heavy usage over long periods of time, or usage by an individual who is psychologically unstable prior to usage, can result in hallucinations, delusions, and auditory misperceptions. Other psychological effects, evident as both long-range effects and as effects during intoxication, include confusion, restlessness, excitement, delirium, disorientation, and clouding of consciousness.

# INTERACTION WITH OTHER DRUGS

*Cannabis* has been found in recent studies to alter the efficacy of a number of common drugs, speeding them through the body and modifying their effect, a fact that makes marijuana use a danger when the user is taking a common prescription drug for an illness or infection.

Besides causing some drugs to lose potency, marijuana interacts with others and can cause a potentially toxic effect when used with caffeine, amphetamines, barbiturates, and tranquilizers.[11]

# RELATION TO MULTIPLE-DRUG USE

About half of those who use marijuana also use other illicit drugs;[12] those who do not use other illicit drugs are usually those who have not been using the drug for a long period of time and who use marijuana in relatively small, infrequent dosages.

A 1974 report by the Secretary of Health, Education, and Welfare stated that "marijuana users as compared to nonusers are more likely to use or have used other, both licit and illicit, psychoactive drugs. The more heavily a user smokes marijuana, the greater the probability he has used or will use other drugs."

A survey taken in 1976 revealed that 85 percent of marijuana users also use hashish; none of the nonusers used hashish. While none of the nonusers used amphetamines, LSD, cocaine, opiates, barbiturates, or tranquilizers, of those who used marijuana three times a week, 52 percent used amphetamines, 51 percent used LSD, 44 percent used cocaine, 24 percent used opiates, 20 percent used barbiturates, and 28 percent used tranquilizers (included in the last two categories were prescription medicines).[13] A study of 367 heroin addicts in the United States revealed that all but 4 had used marijuana before they had used heroin.

Drug studies conducted in Egypt and in the United States reveal that those who use marijuana are also more likely than nonusers to use tea, coffee, tobacco, and alcohol.[14] While nonusers also tended to drink tea, coffee, alcohol, and to smoke tobacco, few used any kind of psychoactive drug.

Several reasons and factors cause marijuana users to move on to more powerful psychoactive drugs. First, and probably the most common, is that once a person uses a drug he becomes involved in a drug-oriented culture and environment; in such an environment, where all kinds of drugs are readily available, peer pressure becomes extremely strong to indulge in still other kinds of drugs.

Second, users who find that they like marijuana sometimes set out to see if there are other drugs they might like — and some set out to try as many drugs as possible.

Third, a marijuana user whose judgment and willpower are reduced can easily be enticed into seeking even greater pleasure than that afforded by marijuana.

Fourth, some users come to enjoy and prefer the variety of sensations afforded by multiple drug use.

Fifth, more powerful drugs tend to mask or offset some of the unpleasant side effects of marijuana; for example, heroin, cocaine, and amphetamines mask the restlessness, sleeplessness, and agitation produced by marijuana and help relieve marijuana's tolerance reaction of a depressed sensual response.

Most respondents questioned in surveys say that they use alcohol with marijuana because of the compounding effect; users of marijuana are twice as likely to use alcohol as are nonusers, and the use of alcohol generally increases rapidly once it is started.

Combination of marijuana with other drugs and with alcohol is dangerous, since drug interactions can render a usually non-lethal dose of a barbiturate or other powerful drug lethal.

# TOLERANCE/DEPENDENCE

It has not been conclusively demonstrated that dependence — a literal physical need for the drug, accompanied by physical withdrawal syndrome when denied the drug — occurs as a result of marijuana usage.[15] The physical withdrawal syndrome — "intense physical disturbances when the administration of the drug is suspended"[16] — has not been observed among marijuana users, even in countries where use has been evidenced for thousands of years.

While physical dependence has not been clearly demonstrated, evidence points to the development of *psychological* dependence.[17] Sixty-five percent of a group questioned in Egypt indicated that they would like to discontinue the use of *Cannabis* "if they could."

While marijuana use does *not* lead to physical dependence, it *does* lead to tolerance ("an adaptive state characterized by diminished response to the same quantity of a drug"[18]). In other words, it takes more of the marijuana to produce the same effects; as the dosage increases, so does the tolerance level.

The first few times marijuana is used, it actually takes *less* each time to produce the same effect; the user experiences more effect with each dose than he did with the last, a phenomenon called "reverse tolerance." The reverse tolerance syndrome, however, only applies to initial usage of the drug and is experienced only with the first few doses.

With continued use of the drug, tolerance develops at a fairly rapid pace. Findings of the Report of the Indian Hemp Drugs Commission revealed that heavy users of marijuana required *four times* the amount of the drug to obtain the same effect as moderate users of the drug. In one experimental study, subjects were given marijuana several times daily for a month in dosages of their own choosing; the subjects increased the dosages steadily (although slowly) over the period of the experiment. While the number of cigarettes smoked daily over the month increased, the pulse rate and other symptoms of euphoria actually decreased, even though the users were slowly increasing the dosage.

Experiments on animals revealed that once tolerance had developed, increasing the drug by one hundred times had little physical effect on the animals that had developed tolerance.

Tolerance to one chemical ingredient of marijuana generally indicates tolerance to the other chemical ingredients of marijuana — for instance, tolerance to delta-9-THC also signals tolerance to delta-8-THC, even when the chemicals are administered separately instead of as parts of the drug — but tolerance to marijuana does not in most cases cross over to tolerance to other drugs (such as morphine or heroin). In some cases, a person may develop tolerance to some effects of delta-9-THC, but not to other effects of the same chemical.

Studies conducted among Eastern groups who have used marijuana for periods of twenty to thirty years reveal that initial doses have increased six times over that period of time.

Subsequent studies have confirmed the rapid development of tolerance among *Cannabis* users.

# THERAPEUTIC USES

As cited earlier, marijuana has been used for centuries in some countries as a medicine, and most of the early uses of marijuana centered around its medicinal properties.

According to some, every human complaint has, at one time or another, been treated by marijuana.[19] A few ancient therapeutic uses of the plant — including use as an analgesic in cases of toothache, dysmenorrhea, rheumatism, and surgery; management of skin infections; management of hysteria and depression; and management of epilepsy and asthma — seem valid today, and many of these possible therapeutic effects are currently being examined.

Until the early 1930s, extracts and fluid extracts of *Cannabis* were on every pharmacist's shelf, and the drug was listed in official directories of approved drugs. Five factors combined in the late 1930s to cause the removal of the official sanction of marijuana as a medicine in the United States:[20]

1. Other medications had been marketed and had been found to be more reliable and effective in treating the symptoms currently treated with marijuana. Those other drugs included morphine and codeine for severe pain, aspirin as a general analgesic, and barbiturates for inducement of sleep.

2. *Cannabis* was too unstable to be considered a reliable medical agent. When exposed to air and light at room temperature, it rapidly lost potency, so by the time it was prescribed it was often inactive. (Even a few days on a pharmacist's shelf reduced the drug's active properties.)

35

3. There was no viable way to standardize the plant cultivation, the plant size and potency, or the plant preparations. Depending on the strain of the plant and the environment in which it was grown, its concentration of delta-9-THC — the most active ingredient — ranged anywhere from 0 to 5 percent. In some cases, the plant material would be completely inert; in other cases, it would be much more potent than the prescriber had anticipated.

4. Because delta-9-THC is not readily absorbed through the intestinal wall, the only really effective method of administration of marijuana is inhalation by smoking — a method prescribers were reluctant to use. Sanctions against women smoking in the early half of this decade rendered it inadvisable for physicians to prescribe marijuana for their female patients.

5. Newspaper stories hawking marijuana as the "devil's weed" appeared throughout the country during the 1930s, and ensuing sensationalism caused marijuana to be classified as a narcotic and caused passage of the Marijuana Tax Act of 1937, making it illegal to grow or possess the drug.

Experiments of old therapeutic uses are bearing out the validity of marijuana as a medication in certain instances, and experiments with new therapeutic uses are indicating that marijuana may have an even broader application in the treatment of disease. Six factors have made it possible for scientists and medical researchers to study the therapeutic effects of marijuana: [21]

1. Methods have been developed to isolate the active principle in marijuana: delta-9-THC. The same methods have enabled scientists to isolate sufficient quantities for medical study.

2. Scientists have discovered that THC essentially reproduces the activity of the plant material, so THC can be used as a pure substance in research studies.

3. Scientists have been able to assay THC and the other cannabinoids in the crude plant preparations and in various body fluids.

4. The National Institute of Drug Abuse has agreed to fund projects designed to clarify the psychological and physiological effects of marijuana.

5. Under a contract from the National Institute of Drug Abuse and through efforts at the University of Mississippi, scientists have been able to develop a reliable source of standardized marijuana; the drug is grown under the auspices of university personnel, and cigarettes used for experimental purposes are standard in dosage and potency.

6. An arrangement between the Food and Drug Administration, the Drug Enforcement Administration, and the National Institute of Drug Abuse has made possible the obtaining of pure sources of *Cannabis* for scientific study.

Marijuana's potential therapeutic uses have been indicated as possibly beneficial in treatment of the following diseases and disorders:

## Glaucoma [22]

Intraocular pressure, which damages the retina and the optic nerve permanently, has been isolated as the cause of glaucoma, a disease of the eye that accounts for 14 percent of all new reported cases of blindness in the United States each year.

Marijuana acts to reduce intraocular pressure in a number of ways:

1. It causes vasoconstriction of the small arteries supplying the ciliary body of the eye, thereby reducing both the capillary pressure and the rate of aqueous fluid secretion.

2. It increases the eye's ability to drain aqueous fluid.

3. It slightly alters ocular tissues to further decrease the rate of aqueous fluid production and to further increase aqueous fluid drainage.

4. It inhibits prostaglandin synthesis (which is not directly related to treatment of primary glaucoma, but which is important in the treatment of secondary glaucoma).

5. It affects a change in the patient's psychophysiologic state, allowing relaxation and euphoria, both demonstrated as significant to treatment.

While marijuana does reduce the amount of intraocular pressure (through cause of the five factors listed above), marijuana *does not* affect visual acuity, visual field, the degree of phoria, stereoscopic perception, refractive error, color vision, clarity of ocular media, or appearance of the eye itself.

Studies indicate that reduction in intraocular pressure is significant; thirty minutes after smoking marijuana, pressure in experimental subjects was reduced from 29 to 34 percent. Studies in Europe indicate that the effect of a single marijuana cigarette on reduction of intraocular pressure is effective for up to one month (depending on dose-tolerance levels).

### Asthma

In normal subjects, marijuana has the tendency to dilate the bronchioles, which during asthma attacks become constricted and make intake of sufficient air difficult or impossible. While several other drugs are effective in bringing about dilation of the bronchioles (especially Mecholyl and Isuprel), THC — the active ingredient in marijuana — lasts longer and tends to require less frequent administration.

Unfortunately, THC is only completely effective when administered in cigarette form — and the smoking of cigarettes is seriously contraindicated for asthma victims due to the irritating effect on the lungs, throat, and bronchial airways. Furthermore, intake of marijuana smoke into the lungs decreases the natural bactericidal activity of the lungs, making them susceptible to bacterial infection (including pneumonia). Asthma, emphysema, and lung cancer have been confirmed as frequent side effects of smoking marijuana cigarettes.

Scientists are currently working on the development of an inhalant spray containing THC that can be used by asthma victims, but research is not progressing rapidly because of the effective asthma medications already on the market.

## Cancer

Marijuana has several applications for treatment of cancer victims. Initial experimental studies have shown that *Cannabis* retards the growth of certain strains of tumors, but THC is generally less effective than other chemotherapeutic agents already on the market for the reduction or retardation of tumor growth. However, scientific research may still lead to development of an effective THC agent that can add to or surpass current chemotherapy chemicals.

Of significant value to cancer victims is marijuana's therapeutic action to control the nausea, vomiting, and loss of appetite that normally accompanies conventional chemotherapy. Standard antiemetics used to treat nausea and vomiting have been completely ineffective against the nausea and vomiting that follows chemotherapy, while initial treatments with marijuana have proven effective in providing complete relief. Also helpful with cancer victims is the tranquilizing, mood-elevating property of marijuana.

## Muscle Spasticity

Marijuana has been shown effective in controlling the spasticity of muscles common with cerebral palsy, multiple sclerosis, and certain kinds of stroke. The ability of THC to reduce and control muscle spasticity is related to its inhibitory effect on the nerve reflexes.

## Epilepsy

Several of the chemical constituents of marijuana have effectiveness as anticonvulsives; cannabidiol seems to be more effective and to have fewer hazardous side effects in seizure-prone individuals than does THC.

Use of marijuana in controlling seizures resulting from

epilepsy needs to be critically monitored by the prescribing physician, since large doses of THC in a seizure-prone individual can cause the onset of seizures.

## Antibacterial Activity

Experiments carried out in Czechoslovakia have proven that certain *Cannabis* extracts can act as an antibacterial agent in reducing the bacterial growth on skin and the mucous membranes.

Marijuana has not been shown effective in controlling bacterial growth internally.

## Hypnotic and Antianxiety Effects

While marijuana has proven useful in providing sedative and hypnotic effects desirable and necessary in certain medical situations, it is not as effective as other preparations currently on the market. Current research may lead to the development of a superior hypnotic agent.

## Treatment for Depression

Since the major reason for nonmedical use of marijuana is for enjoyment of its euphoric effects, scientists began researching the potential of marijuana for the treatment of clinical depression. The use of marijuana has been reasonably successful in some cases, while other researchers have concluded that marijuana is less than effective in the treatment of clinical depression.

Further research needs to be conducted before conclusive evidence can be cited.

## Transplanting/Skin Grafts

Administration of marijuana has proven effective in lessening the body's tendency to reject organ transplants and skin grafts, making it a potentially useful and important drug in the treatment of plastic surgery patients.

Marijuana's beneficial therapeutic actions — reduction of pain, reduction of inflammation, control of convulsions, deadening of nerve impulses, control of nausea and vomiting, and dilation of bronchioles — make it a possible drug-of-importance in the treatment of certain diseases and disorders. However, its undesirable side effects — including transient anxiety, altered perception, interference with normal thought processes, visual and auditory hallucinations, tachycardia, hypotension, hypothermia, hyperglycemia, frequency of urination, diarrhea, and significant reductions in heart and liver weight over a long period of use — call for careful monitoring and close examination of cases in which marijuana is used. In some cases, the undesirable side effects may contraindicate use of the marijuana because they so completely outweigh the drug's benefits.

Still another serious consideration in the use of marijuana as a therapeutic agent is the development of tolerance to the drug; patients who may initially require only a small dose that carries with it few side effects may quickly require larger doses, increasing the occurrence of undesirable side effects.

Currently, those who desire to do research on marijuana's therapeutic effects must receive clearance from the Food and Drug Association and from the Drug Enforcement Administration. All researchers are checked for criminal records — including drug violations — and facilities are inspected for both security and for sanitary conditions. The two governmental agencies require complete records on all research.

# LEGAL STATUS

The first legislation enacted against marijuana in the United States came in 1937 with the Marijuana Tax Act, which made it illegal to possess or grow *Cannabis*. Today, sale and possession of marijuana are considered criminal offenses under federal law; the sale of marijuana is a crime under all state laws, and possession is a crime under most state laws.[23] A few states have eliminated prison as a penalty for the possession or sale of marijuana, and additional states are taking steps to enact similar legislation. Oregon was the first state to entirely eliminate imprisonment as a penalty for personal use of up to one ounce of marijuana; personal use in Oregon is still subject to a fine of $100. Oregon's action came in 1973, and in that same year Texas reduced the penalty for possession of marijuana from two years in prison to six months maximum. The Texas law carried with it a retroactive provision allowing for the release of prisoners serving time for marijuana who had already served the maximum six-month sentence, regardless of the date of conviction.

The variation in approach to marijuana legislation dates to periods when such legislation was first enacted. Possession of marijuana was made a federal crime in 1937, and possession of it carried heavy penalties; those penalties were stiffened twice, and were eventually reduced in 1970 to a maximum of one year in jail, a $5,000 fine, or both.[24] In reality, most common users are not usually prosecuted, with federal law enforcement officials concentrating their efforts on apprehension and conviction of smugglers and major dealers of marijuana (and other drugs).

Penalties under state and local laws vary from state to state, with some states already undergoing reform to lessen the impact of penalty for possession. Again, most law enforcement officials concentrate their efforts on those who sell — not use — the drugs.

Currently underway is a move for nationwide *decriminalization* of possession of marijuana: under decriminalization, a person who possesses marijuana would be subject to a fine but no jail term; in some cases, he would not even have a criminal record as a result of arrest for possession. Basically, possession of marijuana would be placed on a par with traffic violations, as it has already been placed in Oregon. Decriminalization does *not* mean that possession of marijuana would be legal — it simply means that possession would not carry as stiff a penalty. Under decriminalization, marijuana would *not* gain the same legal status as tobacco and alcohol now enjoy.

One of the aspects that has prompted law enforcement officials to move toward decriminalization is the larger number of arrests that occur each year as a result of marijuana possession. In 1965, an estimated 18,815 persons were arrested for violation of state and local marijuana laws; by 1973 — less than ten years later — that figure had jumped to 420,700. The vast majority of those arrests — more than 93 percent of them — were for simple possession of marijuana (usually in small amounts).[25] The result of the increase in arrests was that jails were being filled with young Americans who were forced to mingle with hardened criminals — often violent individuals — in the prisons. Even those who were released from prison after serving a relatively short term were saddled with a prison and criminal record that followed them for the rest of their lives, making it difficult to gain responsible employment.

A campaign was then mounted to prove that marijuana in

small amounts was not dangerous; marijuana violators developed a growing resentment against the government and against law enforcement officials for arrests concerning a matter they did not consider serious.

Out of the growing resentment came Oregon's move to decriminalize marijuana, and Texas followed suit soon after. Other states have since taken decriminalization into serious consideration.

## The Oregon Experience [26]

The effects of decriminalization can be seen by studying the incidence of use in Oregon both before and after laws were changed to remove threat of a jail term from possession of marijuana. Beginning in October 1973, those arrested for possession of marijuana were issued a ticket resembling a traffic ticket and were assessed a fine of $100; possession of less than an ounce of marijuana was no longer a crime punishable by imprisonment in a prison or jail.

One year later — in October 1974 — a survey of 802 Oregon residents eighteen years of age and older was conducted by the Drug Abuse Council. Despite the fact that no criminal penalties were assessed against those possessing less than an ounce, only 72 respondents (9 percent) reported that they were current marijuana smokers — and almost all of them reported that they had started smoking marijuana *before* the decriminalization legislation. Only four of the respondents — 0.5 percent — reported that they had started smoking after decriminalization. These figures tend to refute the arguments of those who claim that decriminalization would lead to widespread use of marijuana.

The respondents in Oregon who reported that they did *not* use marijuana (a total of 91 percent) gave various reasons for not smoking marijuana: they were simply not interested (53 percent); they believed there was a health danger (23 percent); they felt there was still a risk of prosecution (4 percent); they were unable to obtain marijuana (2 percent); they had no reason in particular (9 percent); or they were undecided whether they would begin to use marijuana at some future time (9 percent). Of the 91 percent who did not use it, all but 9 percent had reasons completely unrelated to fear of criminal penalties.

The district attorney for Oregon's Lane County — which includes the city of Eugene — reported that decriminalization of marijuana freed police and other law enforcement personnel to concentrate on apprehension and conviction of criminals involved in violent crime and crime against property.

"When possession of small amounts of marijuana was a crime, we found that police officers allocated a disproportionate amount of their time to the apprehension of those individuals [who possessed marijuana]," the county attorney, J. Pat Horton, reported. "Currently, law enforcement officers spend more time in the area of violent crime and, thus, better serve the community. . . . There is a growing recognition on behalf of citizens in the state of Oregon that police are truly serving the interests of society rather than attempting to enforce unenforceable laws."

Horton added that the relationship between young people and the police has considerably improved, and that criminal courts are significantly less crowded: decriminalization of marijuana removed more than one-third of the cases awaiting trial, freeing the docket for more serious cases awaiting trial.

Organizations currently pressing for full decriminalization include the American Bar Association, the American Public Health Association, the Governing Board of the American Medical Association, the National Advisory Commission on Criminal Justice Standards and Goals, the National Commission on Marijuana and Drug Abuse, the National Conference of Commissioners on Uniform State Laws, the National Council of Churches, and the National Education Association.

On the other side of the coin, those opposed to decriminalization warn that lessening of legal restrictions should be accompanied by a vigorous and widespread campaign to warn potential users of the dangers and health hazards associated with marijuana use. Other concerns include the fear that easing penalties for possession will lead to lessening of penalties for those who sell or grow the drug, and that use of marijuana will spread rapidly.[27]

Opponents to decriminalization further suggest that availability of marijuana has drastically increased since the decriminalization movement began. They also indicate there are real health hazards and dangers, both individually and socially, that would increase from nationwide decriminalization. Perhaps of greatest concern is the fact that a move away from federal penalties toward civil penalties may be interpreted by many that marijuana is safe and approved for use.[28]

# REFERENCES

1. This and the following historical information adapted from Richard E. Schultes, "Man and Marijuana," pp. 59—63, 80—81; "The Use of Cannabis," *The WHO Chronicle* 26 (January 1972): 20—28; and Eugene LeBlanc, "Cannabis: Complex Drug With a Long History," *The Journal*, July 1, 1973, p. 4.

2. Figures obtained from *Marijuana and Health: Fifth Annual Report to the United States Congress from the Secretary of Health, Education, and Welfare, 1975* (Rockville, Maryland: National Institute on Drug Abuse, 1975), pp. 2—3.

3. Robert Rogers, "Reading, Writing, and Reefer," transcript of an NBC News report, December 10, 1978 (the National Broadcasting Company, Inc., 1978), p. 11.

4. "Facts About a Weed Called Pot," *Changing Times*, March 1979, p. 21.

5. "The Use of Cannabis," pp. 21—22.

6. The American Academy of Pediatrics Commission on Drugs, "Effects of Marijuana on Man," *Pediatrics* 56 (July 1975): 1, p. 134.

7. This and the following adapted from "Effects of Marijuana on Man," p. 135.

8. Michael J. Nicar, "Marijuana Use and Abuse," *Chemistry*, January 1979, p. 19.

9. This and the following adapted from "The Use of Cannabis," pp. 22—23.

10. The following information on ʼeffects — both physical and psychological — adapted and condensed from The National Association of State Drug Abuse Program Coordinators, "Marijuana — Health and Legal Considerations," *Grassroots*, August 1977

47

supplement, p. 3; Arthur G. Lipman, "What Are the Pharmacologic Effects of Marijuana?" *Modern Medicine*, March 15—March 30, 1979, pp. 105—106: "Facts About a Weed Called Pot," p. 22; Gerald Milner, "Marijuana and Driving Habits," *Grassroots*, September 1977 supplement, pp. 1—2; Hardin B. Jones, "What Marijuana Really Does," *Listen*, July 1977, pp 1—5; "The Use of Cannabis," pp. 23—27; Harold and Oriana Josseau Kalant, "Cannabis — Some New Answers to Old Questions," pp. 50—61; Ernest L. Abel, "The Relationship Between Cannabis and Violence: A Review," *Grassroots*, July 1977 supplement, pp. 1—10; *Marijuana and Health: Seventh Annual Report to the United States Congress from the Secretary of Health, Education, and Welfare, 1977* (Rockville, Maryland: National Institute on Drug Abuse, 1976), pp. 14—24; Nicar, pp. 20—21; D. Harvey Powelson, "Marijuana: More Dangerous Than You Know," *Reader's Digest*, December 1974, pp. 96—97; "Effects of Marijuana on Man," pp. 136—139; Gabriel G. Hahas, "Marijuana: Toxicity, Tolerance, and Therapeutic Efficacy," *Drug Therapy*, January 1974, pp. 38—43; Vijay K. Mahajan and Gary L. Huber, "Marijuana's Effects on the Cardiopulmonary System, Part I," *Primary Cardiology*, June 1978, pp. 55—58; Victor K. Mahajan and Gary L. Huber, "Marijuana's Effects on the Cardiopulmonary System, Part II," *Primary Cardiology*, July/August 1978, pp. 59—63; Hardin B. Jones, "What the Practicing Physician Should Know About Marijuana," *Private Practice*, January 1976, pp. 35—40; Richard Hawley, "New Proof on Side Effects of Pot," *Provo Herald*, April 26, 1979; Solomon H. Snyder, "Work With Marijuana," *Psychology Today*, May 1971, pp. 37—44; Student Association for the Study of Hallucinogens, Inc., *Capsules*, Volume 6, Number 2 (March—April 1974), pp. 1—4; "Health Aspects of Marijuana Use," *Patient Care*, April 30, 1978, pp. 193—197; and Hardin and Helen Jones, *Sensual Drugs* (London, England: Cambridge University Press, 1977), pp. 215—249.

11. Nahas, pp. 43, 46.
12. Jones and Jones, p. 246.
13. Jones and Jones, p. 247.
14. Ibid.

15. LeBlanc, "Effects of Marijuana on Man," p. 136; "The Use of Cannabis," p. 27; Kalant and Kalant, p. 58.
16. N. Eddy, H. Halbach, H. Isbell, and M. Seevers, "Drug Dependence: Its Significance and Characteristics," *Bulletin of The World Health Organization* 32, p. 721.
17. LeBlanc.
18. Eddy et al.
19. Sidney Cohen, "Marijuana: Does It Have a Possible Therapeutic Use?" *JAMA*, Volume 240, Number 16 (October 13, 1978), p. 1761.
20. Ibid.
21. Cohen, p. 1762.
22. Ivan Goldberg, Michael A. Kass, and Bernard Becker, "Marijuana As a Treatment for Glaucoma," *The Sightsaving Review*, Winter 1978—79, pp. 147—154.
23. *Patient Care*, p. 197.
24. "Facts About a Weed Called Pot," p. 23.
25. "The Private Use of 'Pot' — A Growing Public Issue," *U.S. News and World Report*, April 28, 1975, p. 37.
26. "Marijuana: The Legal Question," *Consumer Reports*, April 1975, p. 266.
27. Jones and Jones, pp. 276—277.
28. National Association of State Drug Abuse Program Coordinators: "Marihuana Health and Legal Considerations," *Legislative Alerts Monthly Reports*, March 15, 1977.